Many men are trying to fi of the biblical instructions for husbands with the same intimidation and confusion as a novice opening his first box of an IKEA do-it-yourself cabinet—impatient, frustrated, and not reading the instructions clearly.

Jeremy Howard identifies with both the new husband who wants to start the race strong and with the experienced husband who falls into a rut yet desires to please the Lord as a leader in the home. In *You're the Husband,* he explains the instructions from the Bible with simplicity. His practical applications for overcoming personal sins, intimidation of leading a more spiritually-competent wife, and ways to lovingly encourage our spouse are given with the encouragement of a personal trainer, wisdom of a tutor, and insight from a counselor.

—STEVEN WONG
Senior Pastor
Fellowship Bible Church, Belmont, CA

Conventional wisdom says that people should write books in the last couple decades of their life after they have gained some experience. This book breaks that mold. Jeremy Howard writes as a young man to young men while the issues of recent marriage are still fresh on his mind. He masterfully navigates through six key principles of leadership in marriage and provides practical homework assignments that will implement God's Word in the husband/leader. Men: read this book!

—PAUL SEGER
Director
Biblical Ministries Worldwide, Atlanta, GA

YOU'RE
THE
HUSBAND

There is a cancerous void that continues to expand in our nation, among a significant mix of generations in America, and abroad. It is a swelling state of division among races and ideologies with no real answer on how to even approach addressing the downward spiral of disunity and tension. The United States has just experienced one of the most polarizing presidential elections in its history, and people from across all generations are crying out to have their voices heard.

Confusion and chaos are being conditioned into our lives as the new normal in even so-called Christian households as husbands, wives, and children are clamoring for answers. Where do we even begin to find answers and hope in this toxic environment we now live in?

In this unstable environment, author Jeremy Howard dares to remind families what it will take to restore that sense of hope and security, and it begins by going back to the basics, more specifically the role of the husband. With a great deal of prayer, sound research, and biblical insight, Jeremy walks the husband through how to be a consistent biblical leader in the home. He does more than simply list facts, but provides a blueprint to equip the husband for leadership in the home. This road map can give insight even to the husband who has no idea where to start. Furthermore, since Jeremy Howard is a millennial, he can address the millennial generation of husbands and men with a boldness that many authors cannot.

Whether you are a struggling husband, or just desire to become better equipped, I highly recommend *You're the Husband* to you as an indispensable biblical resource.

—STEPHEN GOODE
Pastor of Biblical Counseling,
Northside Baptist Church, Charlotte, NC
Author of *Marriage Triage: A Guide to Healing for the Hurting Spouse*

YOU'RE
THE
HUSBAND

A BLUEPRINT FOR LEADING IN MARRIAGE

JEREMY HOWARD

AMBASSADOR INTERNATIONAL
GREENVILLE, SOUTH CAROLINA & BELFAST, NORTHERN IRELAND

www.ambassador-international.com

You're the Husband
A Blueprint for Leading in Marriage

ISBN: 978-1-62020-580-8
eISBN: 978-1-62020-655-3

Cover Design & Typesetting by Hannah Nichols
Ebook Conversion by Anna Riebe Raats

AMBASSADOR INTERNATIONAL
411 University Ridge, Suite B14
Greenville, SC 29601
www.ambassador-international.com

AMBASSADOR BOOKS
The Mount
2 Woodstock Link
Belfast, BT6 8DD, Northern Ireland, UK
www.ambassadormedia.co.uk

The colophon is a trademark of Ambassador

For my wife, Melissa:
May I practice what I preach.

CONTENTS

A mere life of ease is not in the end a very satisfactory life, and, above all, it is a life which ultimately unfits those who follow it for serious work in the world. In the last analysis a healthy state can exist only when the men and women who make it up lead clean, vigorous, healthy lives; when the children are so trained that they shall endeavor, not to shirk difficulties, but to overcome them; not to seek ease, but to know how to wrest triumph from toil and risk. The man must be glad to do a man's work, to dare and endure and to labor; to keep himself, and to keep those dependent upon him. The woman must be the housewife, the helpmeet of the homemaker, the wise and fearless mother of many healthy children. . . . When men fear work or fear righteous war, when women fear motherhood, they tremble on the brink of doom; and well it is that they should vanish from the earth, where they are fit subjects for the scorn of all men and women who are themselves strong and brave and high-minded.

—Theodore Roosevelt, *The Strenuous Life*

THERE'S ROOM TO GROW

Husbands, love your wives,
as Christ loved the church
and gave himself up for her,
that he might sanctify her, having cleansed her
by the washing of water with the word,
so that he might present the church
to himself in splendor,
without spot or wrinkle or any such thing,
that she might be holy and without blemish.

Ephesians 5:25–27

IT STARTED WITH AN OBSERVATION

It's a strange time for me to write a book on marriage. I'm currently 26 years old, I've been married for six years, and I have two young sons. There's a lot of life for me yet to live and there are many things I have yet to learn. What I do have, though, are some lessons learned about Christian marriage, specifically as it relates to Christian newlyweds.

It all started at Calvary University, where I befriended many men who were a joy to know. Looking back, that was a uniquely sweet time in life. Bible college and seminary offer a one-of-a-kind context for Christian young adults. Nearly everyone around me had an earnest desire for truth. By God's kindness, I was surrounded by people who loved the Church and would, in short order, be sent off to serve God in various types of ministries. These guys had a love for God, and many of them met and married godly women while there.

This is when I began to notice certain trends in young Christian relationships. It was easy for me to learn about the issues other couples were having, because many of the men shared their struggles with me as they searched for wisdom. Since I was married before I went to college (I had a whole month under my belt when I started my first class!), many of the men felt comfortable asking me for advice about their marriages. Though I was relatively the same age as them, they saw me as the guy with experience. I would fumble through my answers as I tried to figure things out in my own marriage. But over time, some of the same issues popped up over and over. Through study, prayer, and counsel, I started to figure some things out.

Most of these couples enjoyed the common "honeymoon phase," in which there was little conflict and lots of happiness. As they lived on love, neither the man nor the woman found much to complain about at first. (Side note: There's something about the newness of marital pleasure that tends to numb the sensibilities like nothing else—and I consider that to be quite positive.)

After that, though, reality set in (the timing of this depends purely on every couple's unique context), and each spouse realized that the marriage was going to take work. Many of them came to the understanding that they weren't quite prepared for some of the complexities of their newfound relationships. The men felt especially inept, as the burden of protecting and providing while also loving and listening proved to be a challenge. The women would often get homesick and grow weary of their husbands' expectations.

These difficulties are to be expected in the beginning stages of any marriage. It's a difficult task to transition from caring just for oneself to caring for oneself and another adult sinner. Unfortunately, some marriages nosedive at this point and the couple calls it quits. Though it's incredibly difficult at times, the

God-fearing, gospel-believing couple can push through all misunderstandings and frustrations for God's glory. I'm happy to be able to say that my friends from college were all faithful enough to push through the hangover that follows the honeymoon phase—regardless of how long their struggles carried on.

While being in ministry, I have seen this marital dynamic play itself out multiple times among various couples. Many of the conflicts weren't really the fault of either person; they were the result of a natural sequence of events. Most married people really do seem right for each other. Although I wouldn't exactly call my friends' pairings *kismet*, they certainly came about organically. Boy meets girl, there's chemistry, yadda yadda yadda. So why are there issues? Many of the specific issues will be discussed in the following chapters, but for now I think it's helpful to share another observation about my friends from college.

The more I thought about this marital pattern of honeymoon and then hangover, the more I observed similarities in the backgrounds of the husbands and the wives. Perhaps the most striking and consistent quality was that the men had each been Christians for a shorter amount of time than the women. In fact, many of these men were spiritual toddlers who, like actual toddlers, had learned just enough about the Bible to be dangerous. Most of the wives had been Christians for a decade or more and had parents who raised them that way. Here's a basic overview of most of the couples I knew in college.

HUSBANDS

- Raised in a non-Christian home or rebelled against Christian parents

- Had significant exposure to sinful lifestyles

- Came to know Jesus at an older age

- Eager to get married and start a family

- A Spirit-filled servant of God, ready to lead and get things done

WIVES

- Raised in a conservative Christian home

- Protected from most worldly things

- Had known the teachings of Scripture for years

- Eager to be a faithful wife and mom

- A godly woman needing a new primary spiritual leader in place of her father

As the last two bullets of each list show, the two personalities seem as though they should be a perfect fit. The men appear to be everything that the women are looking for: devoted, hard-working leaders who love Christ. The women are what the men are seeking in a bride: modest, loving, servant-minded women who are full of conviction.

The truth is, these men and women are actually a great fit for each other. But time revealed some deep spiritual issues under the surface of their relationships. Here's what tends to happen.

The wives in these marriages start to realize that they know more about "God stuff" than their husbands. The husbands begin to think that they have entered a competition with their in-laws. The women are shy in the bedroom, and so the men lose their touch for romance. The wives' favorite hobby becomes social media and the husbands get absorbed with TV, video games, or worse (read: porn). More on that later.

That kind of relationship does not have to be—and it should not be—considered normal. God has created men and women for so much more in marriage. It is possible for Christians to have unified, joyful marriages that aren't full of constant frustrations. And it all starts with the man.

This book is a guide for young Christian husbands, answering some of the FAQs before they're even asked.

THE POINT OF IT ALL

It is abundantly clear that God did not design marriage to be easy. He didn't even design it to give us total satisfaction, fulfillment, peace, or joy. Each of those qualities can and should accompany a godly marriage, but Jesus makes it clear where men and women will find their peace: "Come to *me*, all who labor and are heavy laden, and *I* will give you rest" (Matthew 11:28, emphasis added).

This is perhaps the most misunderstood aspect of marriages, Christian or otherwise. Many women think they will be fulfilled or be found in better standing if they could only find a good husband. Many men think they'll become better leaders if they get married and maybe, just maybe, taking on a wife will help them gain victory over their struggles with lust. Those lies never have a shortage of suitors!

But none of those presuppositions are true. God is the only source of sanctification, maturity, and understanding. He has reserved each of those ideals for those who love His word and pursue Him. That's where wisdom is found and where peace is hidden. No one but the Lord can apply complete satisfaction to a restless soul; *total* contentment and fulfillment will never be found in one's spouse.

Marriage is a religious institution rooted in profound spiritual truths, but it is meant only for this Earth. A male sinner is joined with a female sinner in order to reflect God's love for His people, while also providing a means of intimate friendship, sexual satisfaction (see 1 Corinthians 7:9), and multiplication. Marriage is meant to teach both husband and wife what it means to be a child of God, a follower of Christ, and a servant of all. God wants to use every marriage, including yours, to draw people closer to Himself. And that's where I'm coming from in this small book. I hope to make you more aware of spiritual truths as you navigate Christian marriage. It's my hope that whether you've been married three months or thirty years, you'll be challenged and encouraged by the words found here.

Now let's look at what Scripture has to say to young Christian husbands. As we do, I urge you to lay your hearts bare before the Lord and seek what He would have you to do. First, though, please re-read the passage from Ephesians 5 at the start of this chapter before beginning the next.

MANHOOD: DEFINING THE TERM

Be watchful,

stand firm in the faith,

act like men,

be strong.

1 Corinthians 16:13

MANHOOD

When it comes to the subject of growing up, men don't need a long list of vocabulary words to get started. Men just need to know what it means to be a man. Christian men in particular are often unaware of what it means to follow Jesus in a masculine way.

Speaking about this subject, author David Murrow gives great insight for the Church:

> Other religions recognize the tendency of young men to stray and have built elaborate rituals to keep them engaged. Asian Buddhists train every willing boy to become a novice monk. Jews welcome men through the bar mitzvah. Mormons send their young men on a two-year mission. And tribal religions subject adolescent boys to painful, frightening manhood initiations that most Westerners would condemn as abuse. And in Christianity we have . . . the confirmation class. Wow. That'll have the boys lining up.[1]

---

1   David Murrow, *Why Men Hate Going to Church* (Nashville: Thomas Nelson, 2011), 182–183.

Whether or not you're familiar with confirmation classes, you get the point. Traditionally, Christian churches have done a poor job initiating young men into manhood. Most churches have played into the made-up stage of life called the "teen years." The Bible speaks of no such demographic, nor do readers of Scripture find any instance of teen-age people being treated specially in their contexts. Young men are just that—they're men. All Christians should know how to define that simple term in light of biblical truth. And when it comes to Christian manhood, it's best to keep it simple. Here's the definition, the two pillars of manhood: **love** and **responsibility**.

Here's the problem: Most young men don't know how to implement these pillars in their day-to-day lives.

God cares much more about the little details of life than most men ever consider. These details are the minutiae of day-to-day life. Day-to-day life is far different from an eventful snippet of time. Day-to-day life is mundane, routine, and full of seemingly insignificant thoughts and actions; however, it's also where real godliness is displayed.

And marriage, once the newness wears off, becomes like any other segment of day-to-day life. It becomes mundane, routine, and full of (seemingly!) insignificant thoughts and actions. The adventure and excitement give way to familiarity; the unknown gives way to the known. However, true manhood can bring about godliness through a husband's everyday life within marriage. If the man embraces and fosters love and responsibility, he can successfully combat the sins and aggravations that can creep into any marriage, Christian or otherwise.

SETTING A PROPER STANDARD

It's certainly noble to step up in a moment of crisis and display love and responsibility, but for most men it comes naturally. In a moment of real crisis requiring real action, no man worth his weight in salt will stand still.

If a young child is on the street starving, most men will do the loving thing and give the child food. If a building is burning, most men will do the responsible thing and call the fire department. These actions are good, but they're certainly not extraordinary. This virtuous action reflex is more or less evidence of the image of God, not so much the mark of an exceptional man.

Despite mankind's fallen condition, wired into the hearts and minds of every human being is the ability to live out "common grace"—God's way of keeping everyone from killing each other. Men who are civil and do the right thing when it's expected or needed are not extraordinary—they're simply human. But God has not called men to be mere humans. God created all men as humans, yet He calls them to be exceptional, extraordinary, and exemplary. Unfortunately, this concept is completely lost on a huge population of young men in our modern society.

Far too many young men today (even those who have grown up in Christian homes) know only the ordinary kind of love and responsibility. They know that it's right to help a widow when something in her house breaks down; they know they should volunteer to mow the church lawn from time to time; they know that one day they should have a full-time job and a family.

But have these young men been trained how to deal with stress? Do they know how to love a woman? Are they self-starters, who make opportunities and own up to their mistakes? Can they cast a vision, create a budget, or keep a job? Are they honorable? Healthy? Kind? Generous?

Absent in so many young men of the so-called *Millennial* generation are the basic qualities they need to get hired or get married, let alone serve Christ and reflect the gospel. They don't know what it means to go beyond simply showing a few acts of love and responsibility, to living out a life that is full of both. So many of these young men are self-centered, prideful, lazy, and full of lust, but they don't realize it.

Here's their thought process:

I want to feel good.

Playing video games (a diversion from the path of responsibility) and looking at porn (a diversion from the path of love) make me feel good.

Every now and then I'll do something nice so people won't know I'm consumed with making myself feel good.

Now let's restate these thoughts in biblical—i.e., simple, honest, truthful—language.

I'm sinful.

I do sinful things.

I try to hide my sin.

This self-centered thought-life is a monstrous red flag signaling the person's immaturity. Only children and childish adults think like this. It's not how God desires for people to live.

Remember the story in 2 Samuel 11—David's famous sin? David, the great army commander, was on a roll at the time. Israel was like the Yankees of the late 1990s, winning it all every year and with no end in sight. Israel was taking down evil cultures left and right, and David was recognized by the whole world as a military mastermind.

Then it happened. One day in Jerusalem, David got up from a nap and went to the roof of his house to relax. You know what happened next. He saw a beautiful woman, Bathsheba, taking a bath and, of course, his interest was piqued.

At that moment he had to make a decision: whether to be a loving, responsible, and mature man, or to be self-centered and satisfy his desire to feel good. He chose the latter, opting to send his henchmen to pick up the woman and bring her to him. They spent the night together, and she got pregnant.

So David again had to make a decision: whether he would be a loving, responsible, and mature man or be self-centered and fulfill the desire to feel good. He chose the latter again, opting to arrange for this woman's husband to have an imminent death. In a matter of verses, Uriah the Hittite was brought onto the biblical stage and dragged off, stage right.

David was sinful, he did sinful things, and he tried to hide his sin. Though he had great status and rank in the eyes of men, in the eyes of God he was being very childish and selfish.

Unfortunately, this is one of the events for which David became famous. Much of his life was characterized by consistent love and responsibility. He owned up to the sins found in 2 Samuel 11 that were "evil in the sight of the Lord" (v. 27), as Psalm 51 details his dramatic moment of repentance. But the incident with Bathsheba is a perfect example of how men *shouldn't* think.

Giving in to self-centered fantasies leads to a life characterized by sinful wants: lust, pride, greed, and laziness. And when we men choose to worship ourselves like this, we are also rebelling against our Creator.

The answer to the problem of selfishness is to live out love and responsibility, every moment of every day. Let's go positive now and illustrate what exactly is meant by each of these terms.

MOLDING THE PILLARS

LOVE

It's the picture of Jesus we see in Philippians 2:1–8. Be a meek slave. "Do nothing from selfish ambition or conceit, but in humility count others more significant than yourselves" (Philippians

2:3). Sacrifice yourself and your desires. Don't give yourself what you want if there's an opportunity to serve someone else. Make a concerted effort to steamroll your selfish desires and instead bless those around you—especially the annoying people who make your life harder.

RESPONSIBILITY

It's Paul's command in 1 Thessalonians 4:11–12. Discreetly move mountains. "And to aspire to live quietly, and to mind your own affairs, and to work with your hands . . . so that you may walk properly before outsiders and be dependent on no one." He goes on to say in 2 Thessalonians 3 that men should be disciplined and hard-working, they should pay for stuff and earn their keep, they should keep on doing good and call out the lazy guys. It's all about being a good steward of what God has freely given.

These are the pillars of a man. If a man has love and responsibility, he has everything. Then he's eligible for leadership in the home, church, and workplace. He's an all-star. But these pillars don't just show up overnight. It takes diligent effort on the part of God's saint to be a guy who models the life of Christ, reflecting the truths found in Scripture in every facet. How can a young man get started?

- *Pray.* After detailing what a godly life should look like during His Sermon on the Mount, Jesus said, "For everyone who asks receives, and the one who seeks finds, and to the one who knocks it will be opened." (Matthew 7:8). James says, "If any of you lacks wisdom, let him ask God, who gives generously to all without reproach, and it will be given him." (James 1:5). Admit that you don't know anything and plead with God to grant you insight for living a life of Christlikeness.

- *Study.* Men are notorious for not reading instruction manuals. It seems masculine to figure things out without the help of words printed on paper. In the Christian life, however, there's no other way to develop godliness. The Bible must be studied daily. When a woman said that Mary, the mother of Jesus, must be the most blessed woman on earth because of her Son, Jesus answered, "Blessed rather are those who hear the word of God and keep it!" (Luke 11:28b). The psalmist famously said, "Your word is a lamp to my feet and light to my path" (Psalm 119:105). Study Scripture.

- *Seek Out Godly Men.* If dependence on God through prayer and study of Scripture weren't anti-John Wayne enough, this one should be. Ask for help. Godly men who build and establish the pillars of love and responsibility don't do it on their own. They get guidance and accountability from other men—men who are wiser than they are. Proverbs 15:22 says, "Without counsel plans fail, but with many advisers they succeed." It's foolish to think that we can live a godly life on our own without the help of wise men.

A commitment has to be made to prayer, study, and discipleship in order to incorporate love and responsibility into the day-to-day grind of manhood. If there's no such commitment (another sign of immaturity), the pillars of love and responsibility will never be established. It takes a watchful eye and a faithful spirit to be a godly man.

Perhaps this is a good time to reflect on your success (or lack thereof) in this area. Are you known as a loving and responsible man? Are you fooling yourself into thinking that it's okay to be lazy and self-centered? Do you take pleasure in pride, or greed, or lust, or self-righteousness? Is your heart submissive and inclined toward service? What do wise men say about you? Have you asked them for an evaluation?

It all comes back to love and responsibility. This is God's plan for men. And He gives us the power to live it out by His Spirit's power. But we have to choose it, and we have to pick up our cross daily. Your wife (or future wife) will thank you.

A PLAN OF ACTION

Big Idea: Biblical love and responsibility need to become a part of your everyday life.

Assignment: Ask an older, godly man to disciple you. He should be someone whom you already see on a regular basis. Ask your pastor for help if you need to. In your first meeting with him, confess these three things:

- Your weaknesses. Be sure to be honest.

- Your desires. Love and responsibility are paramount.

- Your commitment. Discipleship takes time and effort.

YOU ARE THE LEADER

Then the man said,

"This at last is bone of my bones,

and flesh of my flesh;

She shall be called Woman,

because she was taken out of Man."

Genesis 2:23

IT'S A GIVEN

"Readers shall be leaders" is a phrase often used by teachers to get students motivated to accomplish their studies with purpose. Professors at business schools and seminaries have often used it to encourage the future leaders in their classrooms to build their personal libraries.

Though the phrase undoubtedly includes some amount of truth, a truer statement is this: *"Men* shall be leaders."

When God created the human race, He started with a man. Adam, Scripture says, was created out of the dust of the ground as God breathed into his nostrils, giving him life (Genesis 2:7). After that, God placed Adam in a garden and gave him the responsibility to cultivate it and keep it (v. 15). Then God gave Adam the responsibility of naming all of the animals on the earth (v. 19).

From the start, Man was given the responsibility of management. He was made a steward over the earth and God expected him to lead in creation with diligence and reverence. Following the events listed in Genesis 2 above, Adam was given a wife, because it was not good that he was alone. He named her and God gave him the responsibility of nurturing and keeping her (vv. 23–24). This is the foundation for what is now sometimes referred to as "traditional marriage." That term doesn't need to be controversial because it's marriage *God's way*—He created it! Another way to look at it is to view God as having a design patent on marriage. He's the inventor; it's His intellectual property, so anyone who wants to participate must conform to His specifications. The notion that marriage could be so strictly defined is laughable today to many people in the West, but that doesn't change the fact that God created marriage with a particular function and purpose. His one and only design throughout all of Scripture is for one man to be wed to one woman.

Therefore, any man who desires to be a godly husband must first ask the question, "What does God expect of me?"

Numerous passages in the Bible talk about the relationship that husbands are to have with their wives. In the coming chapters, these five key areas of marital leadership will be addressed and unpacked, using Scripture as a guide:

- *Servant Leadership* – Establishing the mindset

- *Spiritual Leadership* – Pastoring the home

- *Emotional Leadership* – Understanding the weaker vessel

- *Physical Leadership* – Demystifying the bedroom

- *Managerial Leadership* – Steering the ship

MAKE THE EFFORT

Take a moment to consider the following statement: "If I don't lead my family, someone else will." This is truer than most men realize. Generally speaking, women who love God desire to be led.

No matter how many women tout their independence with zeal and gusto, most Christian women know they need male leadership and many of them crave it.

The reason why women desire leadership is quite simple: God designed them that way. Women want to be loved, cared for, and listened to, because the Lord has placed those appetites within them. And those are the qualities that a good leader offers. Men—husbands and fathers—are called to be good leaders, and a good leader is loving, caring, and a good listener.

Striving to lead well takes effort. Although men have been designed to lead, leading well doesn't happen naturally. Men are required to get up each day and seek out wisdom, knowledge, and practical advice in the areas of influence God has given them. In order to be a good leader you must make the effort.

Here's another statement to ponder. "The question is not, 'Am I a leader?' The question is, 'Am I a *good* or *bad* leader?'" If you are a male with influence, you are, by default, a leader. Being a *good* leader is not something that happens by default, though. It takes effort to be an exceptional leader. A man can't live a life of apathy and expect to become extraordinary. Developing good leadership habits is a labor of love. Men are born leaders, but they're called to become *good* leaders.

To be willing to put in the effort that it takes to be a good leader, a man has to realize what's at stake. In his book *Biblical Manhood*, Stuart Scott says this about leadership:

> In any endeavor, there must be an ultimate leader. God chose and equipped Adam for this role. If leadership is a God-given role for men, then each man needs to find the way to lead . . . If all Christian men were taught that it is manly to initiate and lead, there would be not such a lack of leadership in the home and the church.[2]

---

2   Stuart Scott, *Biblical Manhood* (Bemidji, MN: Focus Publishing, 2009), 17–18.

As a follower of Christ, a godly man will treat women rightly and desire to see them grow in their knowledge of and love for the Lord. When his actions are in opposition to those virtues, he becomes a hypocrite in the worst way. Before a man stands up in front of a group of people on his wedding day and pledges enduring love and commitment to his bride, he needs to pledge to God that he will only aid her sanctification—not hinder it. He must acknowledge that his role in his wife's life is more spiritual than it is carnal.

If you've not considered your role in the sanctification of the woman God has given you, now is the time to start. The responsibility is heavy. No longer are you merely responsible for your own growth. You have been charged with the task of helping your wife grow in the Lord. Of course, the Holy Spirit is her perfect Teacher and He will give the increase; but God has placed you in a position of incredible influence and responsibility when it comes to her sanctification.

Ephesians 5:26 states that Jesus sanctifies the church "by the washing of water with the word." God's Word is His means of cultivating holiness in the lives of His people. As this passage states, husbands are to love their wives in that way, causing them to know the Lord better by helping them understand what God has said. This means three things for Christian husbands:

- They must understand what the Bible says.

- They must be changed by it.

- They must use that knowledge and experience to effectively lead their wives.

As with everything else in life that is worthwhile, marriage will consume an incredible amount of time and energy. For the husband to be the leader that God has called him to be, he must start with a commitment to a full-time, life-long process of sacrificial love and selfless effort.

CALLED TO BE PASSIONATE

As I pointed out earlier, a common theme found among Christian couples is the pairing of a "good girl" who was raised in a believing home with a "bad boy" who was raised in a non-Christian home and was saved later in life. Let's examine a few aspects of such a relationship. Positively, the man who has been saved later in life is typically enthusiastic and outgoing concerning his faith. Because he is more in touch with the weight of sin (due to his not-so-distant past), his embrace of God's mercy and forgiveness is typically more noticeable than it is in other Christian men. This energy, which stems from God's saving power, typically runs over into other areas of his life: work, ministries, friendships, etc., making him a desirable mate in the eyes of a young woman trained to take notice of quality Christian men.

This is not to say that men who were never rebellious or exceedingly sinful are always spiritually cold. There are many guys out there who were raised in solid Christian homes who were (or are) just as excited about their faith as their parents. Men like John MacArthur (a pastor's son) serve as a great example of that. However, there seems to be a particular danger to those who are raised in a Christian home. Martyn Lloyd-Jones went as far to say that this issue is at the root of spiritual depression in some cases. He said of depression,

> It is more likely to affect those who have been brought up in Christian homes and families and who have always been taken to a place of worship than those who have not. . . . I would not say that they are not Christians but I am suggesting that they are what I would call miserable Christians, simply because they have not understood the way of salvation, and for that reason all their beliefs and efforts have been more or less useless. They often concentrate on the question of sanctification, but it does not help them because they have not understood justification.[3]

---

3   D. Martyn Lloyd-Jones, *Spiritual Depression* (Grand Rapids: Eerdmans, 1965), 24–25.

This idea is expressed in Luke 7. As Jesus was dining with Simon, a Pharisee, a sinful woman approached the Messiah and wept at His feet (v. 38). She was broken and she knew that Christ could make her whole. She kissed His feet and bared her soul in a very vulnerable moment.

Immediately following her actions, Jesus tells a parable about a moneylender who forgave two debtors completely—one of whom owed ten times as much as the other. When the Lord asked Simon which debtor would love the moneylender more, Simon correctly answered "The one, I suppose, for whom he cancelled the larger debt" (v. 43). Making an immediate application, Jesus turned to the woman and said to Simon, "Therefore I tell you, her sins, which are many, are forgiven—for she loved much. But he who is forgiven little loves little" (v. 47).

Christ was not saying that in order to love Him much, you must go into the world and rack up a long list of sins like the Prodigal Son and then seek forgiveness. After all, from God's perspective, no one is ever "forgiven little." Every single sin is an affront to God's holiness—each one earns the sinner an eternity in Hell—thus, every sinner who is forgiven has truly been forgiven much.

The purpose of this interchange was to challenge the Pharisaical perspective on life and godliness. Jesus's point was that the Pharisee needed to look at himself as being no better off than the woman. The "keeper of the law" needed to understand that he was, in fact, a violator of the law, too, and no good deeds could ever reverse that. This teaching, of course, ran contrary to the philosophy of the Pharisees, and it is because of teachings like this that they were determined that Jesus be crucified.

From the Lord's perspective, whether a person has committed a lengthy laundry list of sins or told only a few "little white lies" here and there, that person can be *greatly* forgiven in Christ. There could never be a ranking system that orders people in line from "most forgiven" to "least forgiven." All people who are saved by

God are delivered from an eternity separated from Him in eternal torment. All people are the "most forgiven" in Jesus. When a man like that Pharisee takes on this mindset and believes in Christ for the hope of salvation, he, like the woman, will love much because of that incredible forgiveness.

Now, thinking back to the Christian men who are younger in their faith: it is understandable how they could be more expressive in their passion for God. They are akin to the woman of Luke 7, who was emotionally broken at the feet of Christ. They are in tune with God's awesome mercy and they are thrilled with this new Spirit-filled life that is marked by the exploration of truth.

On the negative side, however, this man often *does* have a past that is more extensively sinful than that of his wife. Guys who get saved later in life tend to have stories that seem "exceedingly sinful" in comparison to those who were raised in a conservative, sheltered environment. The bride who was raised as a committed Christian will often shudder at the thought of her husband's sexual history, past drug and alcohol use, familiarity with worldly culture, and numerous other issues.

Such a history can undoubtedly lead to challenges and, in turn, possible excuses for the man as he struggles to be the leader in his marriage. A few of the more commonly heard objections and complaints are examined below.

"SHE KNOWS MORE THAN ME"

We men love to know things.

If you're a man, it's likely that you've mastered one or two skills in your life. Each man has his own personal database of the things he loves the most—sports, animals, plants, technology, music, etc.—and he loves to be an authority on that topic.

When it comes to the Christian walk and spiritual matters, it can be difficult for a man who loves the Lord as much as his wife to deal with the fact that he is not quite as knowledgeable or competent as she is (yet). It can also seem very difficult, perhaps pointless, to the man who isn't as well-versed in Scripture (pun intended) as his spouse to try to lead her. It can be extremely deflating when a man realizes that he is not as knowledgeable as his wife in the most important area of their lives. This is a very common roadblock for Christian couples.

The simple fact is that no matter how much intellectual knowledge a Christian man is lacking about the Bible and theology, he is still the leader in his marriage.

Repeatedly in Scripture, believers are commanded to live lives that reflect godliness. And, in the end, the Lord will judge men based on how their faith was lived out (Matthew 25:31–46), as opposed to giving them a final exam to see how much they knew. The Christian life is not measured by a test score, but rather by a life of holiness and faithfulness. So as a believing husband plays "catch up" with his more knowledgeable wife, he can learn from her while also keeping in mind that his life devoted to serving the one, true God is far more important than knowledge alone ever could be.

"SHE DOESN'T UNDERSTAND THAT I WAS DIFFERENT THEN"

Everyone has a past, and everyone carries some kind of baggage into marriage. Sure, some people's baggage weighs more than others'. But it's all still baggage.

One of the hardest things for a young, newly married woman to come to grips with is her husband's past. If the man was a womanizer, party animal, or an angry jerk, the woman may struggle with his past relationships and the bridges he burned over the years. This is a *real* challenge and a delicate subject. Although this is something that needs to be worked out as a couple, here is some advice that should be profitable as you grapple with these thoughts.

- *Be understanding.* When a man's heart is completely changed after years of living in sin, it's very easy for him to understand what has taken place in his life—he's been saved! However, when a man's wife (who has seen only the "A.D." version of him, not the "B.C." version) gains knowledge of his past, her perception may change. The old man of sin that neither of them like has just introduced himself to the wife, though that old man has been totally forgotten to the husband. You must realize this and try to understand things from your wife's perspective. For a man to sympathize with his wife, he will need to be equipped with a great deal of patience, grace, and, above all, prayer.

- *Grow with her.* As a Christian woman is faced with the challenge of understanding the past of the only man she will intimately know for the rest of her life, God is growing and maturing her. As a Christian man is faced with the challenge of being patient and gracious, God is growing and maturing him. The best thing a man can do for his sanctification in this situation is to stay in God's Word while being sensitive to His Spirit's guidance concerning how to speak to and console his bride. Daily Bible reading and frequent discussions with wiser godly men are great tools that the Lord will use to accomplish this goal.

- *Praise God.* It is easy to think negative or sinful thoughts during challenging times. However, the Bible instructs believers to think about honorable things (Philippians 4:8). It says that the Spirit Himself bears witness to remind God's people that they are His children (Romans 8:16). In a difficult time, when a man's wife is struggling to come to grips with the worldly man he once was, it is a great time to praise God for the wonderful work of salvation He performed. Men should hate anything that makes their wives upset—their past sins included! This is a great reminder to praise God for His salvation.

"HER FAMILY IS TOO INVOLVED!"

In the eyes of many young husbands who are new believers, the family of the good Christian girls they love can seem very strange. Several different factors likely distinguish her family from the one in which he was raised. Christian parents are generally more engaged in the lives of their children, and Christian fathers of girls will sometimes be the most involved of all parents. The idea of parents being preoccupied with the details of their children's lives can come across as invasive or even offensive to a man who is not used to it—especially the man who doesn't come from a Christian home. But there are many positives to having in-laws who care. They love their daughter and their son-in-law; they want the best for them; they will likely help in any way possible whenever issues arise.

Some parents do cross the line, though. Each situation must be judged on a case-by-case basis, and the young husband who feels as though his in-laws are in the wrong should seek godly counsel to determine how he should act. Her family may be very involved—they might want to see their daughter frequently, and that will sometimes interfere with the son-in-law's schedule. They may communicate often (daily or multiple times each day) in order to stay up-to-date on what is going on in the lives of their daughter and her husband. They could perhaps cast unsolicited influence into the marriage concerning where the couple will live, how many children they will have, what kind of house they will live in, and what their long-term goals are.

Some Christian parents can be so involved that they keep their daughter from growing into an adult or keep the daughter's marriage from functioning independently. Obviously, there are many opportunities for friction.

The truth is, whenever a mother and father give their daughter away to a man, they are giving that man the responsibility of cultivating and keeping her. It is the husband's job to lead, and he should do so with love and grace even in the midst of others vying for that position. If the woman's family crosses the line, the godly husband must deal with them with grace and truth.

DO TODAY WHAT WILL IMPROVE TOMORROW

Undoubtedly, every man reading this will connect with some aspect of what has been stated to this point. Many men with good intentions have been beaten down by the challenges that accompany biblical marriage. Many men have given up and some have even resorted to a life of sin in order to avoid the hardships that come with godly pursuits. But don't quit. It is possible to be the godly leader God has called you to be.

Simply put, this world is in a leadership drought. Male leadership within the covenant of marriage is extremely lacking. Godly men with the backbone to stand up for their convictions while maintaining the gentle spirit needed to love a woman are few and far between. Now is the time to buck the trend.

Commit to doing today what will improve your tomorrow. If redeemed men around the world will turn to God with a sincere heart and say, "I am going to do whatever it takes to lead my wife the way You want me to," He will honor that. He has supplied men with His own divine guidance and power to lead in marriage. If Christians will depend completely on Him only, laying hold of the tools He has provided (Ephesians 6:10–20), they will be empowered to do His will. If this were to play out globally in husband-and-wife relationships, the Christian faith would be supplied with one of the greatest evidences of its authenticity. We men are not given enough days to start doing tomorrow or the next week everything we need to be doing—the time is now.

In the next chapter we will examine some of the specific details concerning what male Christian leadership looks like within the marriage covenant. For now, it is enough to realize that you, the man, are given the responsibility of leadership. The first step in living the life God wants you to live begins with accepting this responsibility.

A PLAN OF ACTION

Big Idea: Men are leaders by default. Husbands are called to shepherd their wives, no matter how difficult it might seem.

Assignment: Start living like a leader. Ask your wife (or bride-to-be) the area(s) in which you need to improve the most. Women usually feel like this is a lose-lose situation for them, so be very kind and clear. If necessary, tell her to think it over for a day or two and let you know in a letter or email.

Evaluate the feedback you get, connect with a godly man who is awesome in that area, and ask him to teach you/keep you accountable/pray for you.

You should be fired up about this issue! If it matters to her, it absolutely matters to you.

YOU ARE THE SERVANT-LEADER

Therefore a man shall leave his
father and his mother
and hold fast to his wife,
and they shall become one flesh.

Genesis 2:24

SERVANT:

ESTABLISHING THE RIGHT MINDSET

If asked, most people could name individuals in their lives who are more selfless than themselves. Whether the humble person is a mother, father, brother, sister, or friend, everyone cherishes a truly selfless person. God gave mankind the chief example of selflessness when He took on human flesh in the person of Jesus. The way Jesus lived His life—and the way He led His followers—was marked by revolutionary, sacrificial, servant-leadership. The world is still in desperate need of this example and there is no better place to implement it than within the covenant of marriage.

The term *servant-leadership* encompasses several ideas. The most basic idea is that the leader must not consider himself and his wants to be of utmost importance. In fact, it is impossible for a person to be a servant when he places more value on his own interests than the interests of others. Philippians 2 lays this out, as the Holy Spirit says through Paul, "Do nothing from selfish ambition or conceit, but in humility count others more significant than yourselves." (v. 3). In the book of Matthew, Jesus challenged His disciples to be completely selfless. He said, "If anyone would come after me, let him deny himself and take up his cross and follow me" (Matthew 16:24). It's key to note exactly what Christ said: "he *must*"—an imperative. God is stating that a prerequisite for following Him is a complete abandonment of self-interest. This message is the direct antithesis of the world's, which encourages self-absorption.

The word "deny" (Greek, *aparneomai*) means "to disown, repudiate, or disregard." As Christ spoke to His disciples that day, conveying this message to them, He was not inviting them to merely put selfish ideas out of their minds. He challenged them to *completely disown* their interests for the sake of His. Before they could understand what it meant to live the Christ-life, they had to understand what was standing between them and their Savior: self. It was impossible then—and it's still impossible today—to let God drive while we are sitting in the driver's seat. We must die to self.

To put it in the context of marriage, there's no other way to be a devoted husband than to do away with self. In order to be faithful, gracious, forgiving, and kind, you have to put yourself last. Your interests must pale in comparison to the needs of your wife. As a married man, following Christ means that serving your wife is of utmost importance. If you reach a new level on the latest Xbox game but don't pray with your wife, the Holy Spirit is grieved.

At another point in His ministry, Jesus addressed the crowds saying, "If anyone comes to me and does not hate his own father and mother and wife and children and brothers and sisters, yes, and *even his own life*, he cannot be my disciple" (Luke 14:26, emphasis added). The word "hate" (Greek, *miseo*) means "to detest, to love less, to esteem less." Jesus was not trying to cause a war between family members just for the sake of a feud. He was calling people who wished to follow Him to love Him more than they loved the most important people in their lives—including themselves. A radical devotion to God beckons a radical denial of self.

The ultimate, bottom-line truth behind Christ's call to discipleship is that no person can be a *true* servant if he counts himself equally (or more) important than the subject of his servitude. If a man desires to live out the gospel, he must consider himself unimportant in light of the God he serves. If he wants to live humbly and generously, he must be selflessly mindful of others. And though it may seem counterintuitive, if he wants to be a leader he must emulate the qualities of a slave.

God has called men to be servants; they are called to be diligent stewards of His grace. His blessings are to be used to serve others in the freedom that comes with the gospel of Christ. As God said through Peter, "Live as people who are free, not using your freedom as a cover-up for evil, but living as servants of God" (1 Peter 2:16). John MacArthur rightly sums up this same thought in his book, *Slave*, when he wrote "To be a Christian is to be Christ's slave."[4] He went on to explain, "Such slavery is the only freedom."[5]

KEEPING HER NEEDS FIRST

Though living as a slave might be difficult, translating the mindset of servanthood into the context of marriage is not at all difficult. In fact, the Bible expressly commands that husbands should sacrificially show love toward their wives. In Ephesians 5:25, God says, "Husbands, love your wives, as Christ loved the church and gave himself up for her."

This frequently-used verse is often presented without proper commentary concerning the weight of the command. As Paul directly addresses husbands in this verse, he cites Christ's love for His

---

4   John MacArthur, *Slave: The Hidden Truth about Your Identity in Christ* (Nashville: Thomas Nelson, 2010), 22.
5   Ibid., 222.

church as the standard for a man's love toward his wife. And how did Jesus show His love for the church? *He gave Himself up for her.*

In John 15:13, Jesus says, "Greater love has no one than this, that someone lay down his life for his friends"—and that's exactly what He did! His sacrificial love provided salvation for everybody. This salvation is rooted in God's covenantal lovingkindness and possessing salvation is absolutely necessary for men to escape the wrath they have earned for themselves (Romans 6:23). This is the gospel in its most basic form—Christ came into the world to save sinners and He did so by dying for them (cf. 1 Timothy 1:15).

Mankind has always existed in a helpless state. Because of the sin that exists in every individual and the evil that is propagated by the world as a whole, men (and women) are unable to help themselves to be better. Apart from a work that is not of themselves, a perfect sacrifice, no man is able to be saved from the judgment that he deserves. But because "God so loved the world" (John 3:16), He "sent his only Son into the world, so that we might live through Him" (1 John 4:9). Romans 5:8 says it this way: "God shows his love for us in that while we were still sinners, Christ died for us."

If God were not completely loving, the sacrifice of Jesus never would have been made. If Christ had not put others' needs ahead of His own, mankind would still be in a state of helplessness. However, since Jesus was mindful of the world, the world now has hope. Philippians 2:7–8 says that Jesus Christ "emptied himself, by *taking the form of a servant,* being born in the likeness of men. And being found in human form, he humbled himself by becoming obedient to the point of death, even death on a cross" (emphasis added).

The apostle Paul had all of this in mind when he penned the words of Ephesians 5:25 quoted above. The Holy Spirit, who moved Paul to write the command, absolutely purposed the weightiness of the words. A man who has decided that he is mature enough to marry a woman must be humble enough to serve her sacrificially. Jesus entered the world as humbly as He could have and lived a life more sacrificially than anyone who has ever lived. He should be every Christian man's primary Teacher in every part of life—including the sphere of marriage.

To love your wife as Christ loved the church is to be willing to die for her *daily*. In accordance with the concept of manhood, most guys understand sacrificial love in big picture terms. Most men will fiercely protect their families if an intruder comes in the middle of the night. Most men would drop everything they're doing and rush to the scene if their wives were in a bad car accident. But do these same men readily help out around the house? Do they change diapers? Do they listen to their wives and take the time to give them godly counsel? Are they willing to shut off a glowing screen in order to attentively shepherd the woman God has given them?

Every husband needs to implement the idea of sacrificial love in all areas. The Bible uses the Greek word *agape* (love) to explain this concept. *Agape* is a purely biblical word in construct and concept. It's a word that retains a meaning only God could generate. Selflessness, sacrifice, and unconditional devotion are the anthems that this word sings out and husbands are specifically told to practice it.

If most men are honest with themselves, they have no idea why God graced them with their wonderful wives. The fact of the matter is that He did and they're expected to love these women as Christ loved the church and gave Himself up for her.

LEADER:

TAKING RESPONSIBILITY

Husbands are responsible.

That sentence can be viewed two ways: (1) Husbands should live out the characteristics of responsible people, or (2) Married men, by default, own up to the issues that arise in their marriage.

Both statements are true.

In the opening chapters of Genesis, life on earth was described as "very good" (1:31). However, in chapter three, things took a turn for the worse. A serpent, Satan himself (Revelation 12:9), entered the garden and deceived Eve. The Devil twisted God's Word (Genesis 3:1), lied (v. 4), and pitted the woman against her loving Creator (v. 5). Eve then disobeyed God by taking of the fruit she was commanded to avoid and "she also gave some to her husband who was with her, and he ate" (v. 6). After that, the two covered themselves and hid from God (vv. 7–8).

Every single word of Scripture has been placed there intentionally by its Author, and Genesis 3 proves just that. Notice that the husband is described as being "with her." This adds so much more context to the story. Adam was present during this entire incident. Without the Holy Spirit's inspiration, it would have been impossible to know this. He was right there *with her.*

Adam, the first created human, the man who was given the responsibility of nurturing the first woman, stood by his wife while she was deceived and then took part in the sin she committed. He did not protect her; he subjected her. He did not stop her; he joined her. He did not correct her; he hid her. He completely failed as a husband.

When God entered the scene in the garden to address their sin, He did not call out for Eve, or both of them for that matter—He called for Adam, the husband, specifically. "Where are you?" God said to the man (v. 9). In his shame, Adam replied, "I heard the sound of you in the garden, and I was afraid because I was naked, and I hid myself" (v. 10). Eventually God punished the man by causing his work to be hard and his livelihood difficult. The woman was given painful childbearing and the desire to rule over her husband, though he should rule over her. Life has never been the same since.

Now, in the 21st century, husbands are still responsible. They are expected by God to live out the qualities of a responsible person as well as owning up to the issues that pop up in their own households. A husband's responsibility extends far beyond putting on his pants each morning and taking out the trash. A man of God should feel an obligation to cultivate and keep his wife the way the Lord has commanded. Here are some of the basic ideas outlining what it means to take responsibility.

DO WHAT IT TAKES TO PROVIDE

Somewhere between the Garden of Eden and the invention of the latest video game consoles, it became acceptable for guys to live in their parents' basements, not go to work, and be addicted to the internet (read: "porn"). These kinds of guys are boys who never grew up. They never went through a rite of passage to become a man. They take on no responsibility, show no initiative, and have zero motivation. They aren't creating anything, leading anyone, or contributing to society. This isn't God's will for them.

It's hard to believe that so many of these sloths-who-can-game even exist. If the Darwinians (who control much of American society) actually implemented their philosophy of "survival of the fittest," the 20-something male would become an endangered species. Many strong words need to be said to these individuals, but all of that should be saved for a different book.

Unfortunately, when a guy who fits the above description somehow winds up in a marriage, his outlook on life often doesn't change. The only real difference in his life is that he now bums off of his wife instead of his mother. His spouse struggles to get him motivated while she suffers under the total lack of servant-leadership in their marriage. He thinks he's cute while everyone else (except his parents and fellow sloths) wonders when he'll grow up.

As previously stated, work isn't always fun. Part of the curse was to make work hard for mankind. However, part of servant-leadership is to do what it takes to provide. This includes going against a natural tendency to sleep in, lounge around, and waste the day away by focusing on our self. The truth is that men *need* to work.

Paul took the idea of earning a living and serving others very seriously. In his second letter to the Thessalonians, he said this:

> Now we command you, brothers, in the name of our Lord Jesus Christ, that you keep away from any brother who is walking in idleness . . . For even when we were with you, we would give you this command: If anyone is not willing to work, let him not eat. For we hear that some among you walk in idleness, not busy at work, but busybodies. Now such persons we command and encourage in the Lord Jesus Christ to do their work quietly and to earn their own living.
>
> 2 Thessalonians 3:6a, 10–12

This charge was made openly to the men of Thessalonica and the apostle even went on to say, "If anyone does not what we say in this letter, take note of that person, and have nothing to do with him, that he may be ashamed" (v. 14).

So if men, generally speaking, are all called to work, earn a living, and serve other people, how much more should husbands seek to provide for their wives with whom God has blessed them? Providing is a vital part of taking responsibility. In another place, Paul put it plainly: "But if anyone does not provide for his relatives, and especially for members of his household, he has denied the faith and is worse than an unbeliever" (1 Timothy 5:8). It's a big deal.

TAKE ALL OF THE BLAME AND NONE OF THE CREDIT

John Wooden once said, "A strong leader accepts blame and gives the credit. A weak leader gives blame and accepts the credit."[6] In contrast to that virtuous statement, Michael Scott, the lead

---

6   John Wooden, *Wooden on Leadership: How to Create a Winning Organization* (New York: McGraw Hill, 2005), 29.

character on the TV show *The Office*, once said to his CFO, "I'll be honest with you . . . I do want the credit without any of the blame." It's easy to point fingers when things go wrong. In a marriage that is struggling to survive, a husband or wife might place all of the blame on their spouse. "If only he did this," or "If she would only be like that," are common thoughts that run through the mind of a married person who thinks his or her significant other is at fault. Though it is incredibly tempting to take part in such a childish argument while in the flesh, at the end of the day, God comes looking for the man. Remember in Genesis when the man and the woman were in the garden: Eve was deceived, then Adam sinned with her (cf. 1 Timothy 2:14), but the first person God came looking for was Adam.

Husbands need to consider their marriages as precious and as fragile as the first man-woman relationship found in the opening chapters of the Bible. If this delicate union's success or failure is tied directly to the husband, its leader, then he needs to step up when things go south. Just like a great basketball coach, a man should be willing to accept the blame when his team is not functioning like it should. It's his responsibility to recognize the issue, own up to it, and fix it. He is the leader.

If your wife is making the majority of your family's decisions, you're doing it wrong. If something goes awry in your family and you tell yourself or others that it was completely her fault, you're not taking proper responsibility for your family. You're a man. God has made you and called you to be out front, leading the pack, making decisions, and taking blame for things that go wrong.

If a project fails, if someone sins, or if mistakes are made, use the energy you have to fix what's broken, make a new plan, and move forward. If you use your energy to disparage your wife, may God have mercy on your soul. You deserve a punch to the head.

A servant-leader not only *takes* all of the blame, but he also *gives* all of the credit. In most marriages, there are just as many good things happening (if not more) than there are bad. The children may be excelling in life, the house might be clean and paid for, and perhaps life is running as smoothly as possible. The good husband attributes all the credit for that to God's grace and he praises his wife's efforts.

Proverbs 31 is famous for recognizing the godly woman, explaining what makes a woman noble in the eyes of God. "Her children rise up and call her blessed; her husband also, and he praises her: 'Many women have done excellently, but you surpass them all'" (vv. 28–29). Notice the action the husband takes in relationship to his wife. He *praises* her. Though there are probably (and hopefully) some qualities of a righteous wife's life that come from her husband's leading, the man should not take a fleshly pride in that. A servant-leader is not concerned about his own interests; he is more concerned about the needs of others. A good husband praises his wife. He is a servant.

KEEP INVESTING IN HER

It's easy for many men to slip into a type of "maintenance mode" in their marriages. After the honeymoon period fades away, the still-newlyweds begin feeling comfortable with each other. They're so comfortable, in fact, that they don't spend as much time investing in one another as they did before. The little things that they used to do for each other become memories of a past romance. As long as nothing is going horribly wrong in their marriage, they'll say to themselves and others that "everything is fine."

Men—husbands, servant-leaders—are called to so much more than merely maintaining the status quo and being "good enough." A husband who cares about his wife and the standard that God has set before him won't hesitate to keep investing in his spouse. Peter describes it this way: "Husbands, live with your wives in an understanding way" (1 Peter 3:7).

A man who lives with his wife in an understanding way will listen to her, counsel her, give her advice, and treat her gently, with conviction and love. In the following chapters, each of the qualities that makes a husband "understanding" will be discussed further, but for now it is important to realize that a marital leader must be one who invests in his bride.

To invest in your wife, you must take to heart the responsibility of shepherding. Jonathan Edwards said, "Every Christian family ought to be as it were a little church, consecrated to Christ, and wholly influenced and governed by His rules." The pastor of this "little church" is certainly the husband. You have been tasked with the responsibility of watching over your home flock, aiding the maturation of your wife and children, and keeping them as a priority.

Additionally, it wouldn't hurt to memorize the second half of this quote from Martin Luther: "Let the wife make the husband glad to come home, and let him make her sorry to see him leave."

THIS IS SERIOUS BUSINESS

Most people have heard the saying, "Behind every good man is a good woman." But what if the phrase were reversed to speak of marriage specifically by stating, "Behind every *bad marriage* is a . . . "? What would the answer be? According to Scripture, the answer is an irresponsible husband.

This is not to say that wives can't be at least partially responsible for bad marriages. However, a man who is completely devoted to God's way of marriage will do all that he can to keep things biblically sound. When a man fulfills his godly duty in this way, he not only honors God but he makes it easier for his wife to follow him.

It is impossible for a man to consider his marriage too seriously. When a man and woman stand up before God and witnesses to pledge their love to one another in a covenant designed by their Creator, from that point on their lives are taken to another level.

No longer is a man responsible only for himself, but he is also accountable for the relationship he has with another person—who is a sinner just like him. No longer is his main responsibility to worry about his own schedule and his personal goals; he is now charged with the task of sacrificially loving one of God's own daughters. This is serious business.

As husbands, men should desire to lead their wives; this is done by serving them and putting their needs first. It is incredibly important to remember that when a husband lives out his marital duty as a servant-leader, he is imitating his Savior, seeking to become more Christ-like through a covenant created by his Lord. Marriage is about love, and perfect love is found only in Jesus.

A PLAN OF ACTION

Big Idea: In order to lead in your marriage, you must be a slave. In order to be a slave, you must invest in the woman God has given you.

Assignment: Become an expert at serving your wife. Do this by implementing these four habits:

- Ask, "What can I do for you?" a lot. Ask it multiple times a day. When she gives an answer, get up and do it.

- Ask, "What can I be praying about for you?" multiple times a week. Then pray about those things for her and follow up with her.

- Only *praise* your wife to others. Don't let a negative word come out of your mouth when she comes up in conversation. Slaves who trashed their masters had a bad thing coming to them. Same rule applies here. If there's something that you think she needs to work on, it's your job to talk to her one-on-one. Don't dare complain about her to someone else.

- Wash her feet regularly. Literally. Grab a big bowl, add warm water and soap, find a washcloth and some lotion. Take off her shoes and socks, sit at her feet and wash them. You're thinking, "This is going to be terribly awkward." It's because you haven't done it before. Read John 13:1-17 for encouragement. Really dwell on verse 17. You man enough to do this?

As always, get accountability on these issues.

YOU ARE THE TEACHER

So when the woman saw that the tree

was good for food, and that it was a delight

to the eyes, and that the tree was to be desired

to make one wise, she took of its fruit and ate,

and she also gave some to her husband

who was with her, and he ate.

Genesis 3:6

TRAGEDY IN THE GARDEN

Adam's sin in the Garden of Eden was introduced in the last chapter. He passively subjected Eve to Satan's lies, he joined her in her sin, and he hid from God with her. He messed up—big time.

Where exactly did Adam go wrong? It seems as though it started somewhere between Genesis 2 and Genesis 3. The man and woman were naked and happy, content with the relationship that God had created (2:25). Suddenly, Satan entered the picture (3:1) and began to deceive Eve, all the while her husband kept his mouth shut. Adam was so quiet, in fact, that the reader would not even know that he was present, were it not for verse six, which says he was "with her."

Not only did this event reveal that Adam failed to *protect* his wife the way he should have—it implies that he had failed to *teach* his wife the way he should have.

To unpack this hypothesis, it is helpful to fast-forward to the New Testament, where Paul gives some insight into what role a husband plays in his wife's spiritual growth. As the apostle wrote his first letter to the Corinthian church, some of his reasons for writing to them were to clarify gender roles, discuss marital issues, and establish orderly worship in the church.

First Corinthians 14:35a says of women, "If there is anything they desire to learn, let them ask their husbands at home." This sentence was penned well after Adam and Eve were sent out of Eden, yet a basic principle is established here: a woman's husband is to be the spiritual leader and teacher of the home.

In 1 Timothy 2:11–14, Paul talks about the specific incident that led to original sin and what it means for today: "Let a woman learn quietly with all submissiveness. I do not permit a woman to teach or exercise authority over a man; rather she is to remain quiet. For Adam was formed first, then Eve; and Adam was not deceived, but the woman was deceived and became a transgressor."

Eve's gullibility in the Garden was the proof for the points Paul made in his letters that were written thousands of years later. As God's first-designed humans, men are called to be responsible spiritual leaders and women are their help-mates. This is what the Lord wanted from the very beginning (cf. Gen 2:20); however, both Adam and Eve failed to fulfill their spiritual duties in Genesis 3. Adam was not behaving as a passionate spiritual teacher in his union with Eve, as was evidenced by the ease with which Satan deceived her.

God had given the man only two commands: Eat of every tree except for one, and be fruitful and multiply. That was the entire doctrinal statement given to humanity up to that point. Therefore, as the designated teacher of the first man-woman relationship, Adam had the responsibility to pass that information on to his wife. One of these commands, of course, Eve broke.

It would not be totally fair to say that Eve's sinful action ab-solutely means that Adam failed to teach her the rule—though that is a real possibility. A man is not able to force his wife to live righteously. What can be inferred, though, is that in the moment of Eve's transgression, Adam was apathetic. The actions chosen by Adam and Eve proved that when humans have the power of choice, they choose to rebel against God. Adam and Eve rebelled by rejecting their God-given roles in order to obey their own lusts. Adam gave in to the sin of apathy and laziness, both of which are rooted in pride.

It can be assumed that no man would stand idly beside his wife if she attempted to take her own life. He would likely instinctively scream out, "No! Stop!" in an effort to protect her from destroying herself. In the same way, a godly husband will protect his wife from sinful decisions. That is what a good teacher does—he recognizes evil, teaches against it, and works to expel it.

Genesis 3:6 destroys any chance that Adam ever had for the *Godly Husband of the Year Award.* Though he may have recognized the evil in Eve's consumption of the fruit, he did not teach against it or encourage her to avoid it. As a result, the human race fell. The Lord expects so much more out of His teachers.

IT MAY BE TIME FOR A DIAGNOSTIC CHECK

A rocky relationship with Christ in a man's life greatly hinders his relationship with his Christian wife. One of two things will likely happen in that situation: the woman will either excel in her faith, growing in her sanctification and effectively leaving her husband behind, or she will be dragged down to her husband's level, following his example. Neither one of those situations honors God. Only the husband can right the ship.

Being a good leader starts with being a good follower and being a good teacher starts with being a good student. As men humble themselves by submitting their lives to Christ's authority, they will grow by His grace and through His Word. Men cannot be good teachers unless they are being taught by the greatest Teacher. For the Christian men, another Helper has been sent for them. He comforts, teaches, counsels, and illumines Scripture.

> For who knows a person's thoughts except the spirit of that person, which is in him? So also no one comprehends the thoughts of God except the Spirit of God. Now we have received not the spirit of the world, but the Spirit who is from God, that we might understand the things freely given us by God.
>
> 1 Corinthians 2:11–12

This passage goes on to say that without the Holy Spirit, men would not be able to comprehend the things of God (v. 14). Thus, saved men must rely on Him to teach them the doctrines that are expressed through His Word. Being a good student in this way equips husbands to teach their wives. If this link in the chain is missing, the man's role as teacher dissolves and he is left with nothing more than self-help books and his own thoughts, which are, of course, disastrous options (Leviticus 10:1–3, Jeremiah 17:9).

This should be encouraging to the husband who knows very little. Your role as the spiritual teacher in your marriage is not determined by the score you get on a theology test. When it comes to teaching, God requires only that Christian husbands humbly learn from Him while they lead their wives. Jesus said it this way:

> Abide in me, and I in you. As the branch cannot bear fruit by itself, unless it abides in the vine, neither can you, unless you abide in me. I am the vine; you are the branches. Whoever abides in me and I in him, he it is that bears much fruit, for apart from me you can do nothing.
>
> John 15:4–5

Have you ever considered this passage in light of marriage? Many men struggle in marriage as they seek to do all of the things they know God has called them to do. Jesus's solution for men is that they should abide in Him. This means that a husband should rest under the authority and wisdom of Christ and His Word, knowing that He is able to make a marriage what He wants it to be. Apart from the Son of God, you can do nothing.

BE TEACHABLE; BE A TEACHER

Tiorio is credited with the saying, "You will never be a leader unless you first learn to follow and be led." That statement is so true. However, it should be noted that there is a big difference between a man acknowledging he needs a teacher and a man actually submitting to someone else's teaching and leadership.

As stated, the Holy Spirit is the greatest Teacher for believers who want to understand the things of God. Additionally, the Lord has granted His children other teachers. Titus 1 outlines the roles of elders in the church. In chapter two, Paul explains how older men and women in the church are supposed to teach the younger men and women that which is godly and true. Husbands must seek out the older and wiser men—the spiritual authorities in the local church—for guidance in spiritual matters.

Here is a tested principle: if a man is not willing to submit to the godly authorities in the church, he will not be able to develop into a godly leader himself. This kind of man is dangerous because he considers his own opinions to be all-sufficient and all-wise. Scripture makes it clear that nobody should think that way. Men who fit this description are likely terrors at home as well. They have gone rogue spiritually and consider themselves to be brilliance personified. Ironically, they don't know that there's so much they don't know.

Humility and teachability go a long way in spiritual matters. As long as a man is willing to sit under the teaching of a wiser and more knowledgeable man, he has no ceiling on his Christian potential. Every believer has something to learn, and God has designed His church specifically for the equipping of one another (Ephesians 4:11–12, 1 Peter 4:10–11). If a man wants to be a godly husband, he will consider the teachers in God's church as invaluably precious.

WHOM WILL SHE LISTEN TO?

A woman does not cease to learn just because her husband fails to teach. Just like every other person on the face of the earth, the wife who isn't being led still desires to look up to someone and be instructed, encouraged, and empowered. If she doesn't get this from her husband, she'll get it from someone else. Someone will *always* be teaching your wife. Don't you want that person to be you?

Thinking back to the Garden of Eden, as Eve stood next to her quiet, passive husband, she received instruction not from Adam, but from the serpent. It wasn't that the woman was necessarily out looking for a leader to replace her failing husband, but the moment a figure arose to provide her with instruction, encouragement, and empowerment—she listened. There will always be teachers (whether good or bad) ready to provide women with information and direction. It's up to the husbands of these women to protect them.

Just as pastors are encouraged to hold fast to correct doctrine for the sake of the church (1 Timothy 4:2–5), husbands, the pastors of their homes, are encouraged to do the same for the sake of their wives (Ephesians 5:25–27). In turn, women are encouraged to submit to their husbands (1 Peter 3:1) as the church is called to submit to its leaders (Hebrews 13:7). God has given specific people specific roles for specific purposes and if everyone submits to

His plan, He will ultimately be pleased with the outworking of His own design.

"TO BOLDLY GO WHERE NO MAN HAS GONE BEFORE"

Many Christians are raised in homes where there is no real spiritual leadership. Whether the father was passive, apathetic, domineering, or flat-out opposed to God, his children were raised without a godly father. It's up to the Christian guys who came out of these households to change the course of their family's future generations. Just one man can change the entire family tree from that point forward. If his parents are still alive, he can even lead them to Christ through the gospel. God can use him to completely change everything.

What this means for the Christian man is *devotion*. He must be devoted to his God, his church, his wife, and godliness. This can play out in several different ways. In some Christian families, the husband calls everyone around the dinner table each day to have a family devotional. In other families, the man may not be as formal in his day-to-day spiritual leadership. There are different methods for being the spiritual leader, though there is only one basic principle: lead well.

At the end of a Christian husband's life, God will not question him, saying, "For what reason did you not read *Our Daily Bread* to your children each day?" The Lord cares about the man's faithfulness to his family ministry. In whatever way that manifests itself, it is important that the husband commits himself to being the responsible spiritual leader for his household.

A PLAN OF ACTION

Big Idea: God has given you the responsibility of teaching your wife and this should be a major part of your marriage. Your authority is Christ and His Word; seek to learn from the leaders in the church.

Assignment: Adam's issues were traced back to his heart and his eyes. He didn't have the heart of a teacher or the eyes of a passionate coach. He wasn't committed to truth or opportunities to correct wrongdoing. You're called to be different.

- Develop a heart for good doctrine. Love the Bible that God wrote and generously gave to you. Find a good teacher and get him to mentor you and show you how to be a better teacher. Grab a guy who is really fired up about teaching good stuff and tell him you want that same kind of passion. Ask him to help you with that.

- Develop eyes that see things in two places: (1) In Scripture (2) In your home. You need to see things in Scripture so that you know what the truth is. You need to see things in your home so that you know how some things might be out of alignment with God's Word. Care about Scripture and care about seeing it lived out under your roof.

YOU ARE THE ROCK

Then the man and his wife heard

*the sound of the L*ORD *God as He*

was walking in the garden in the cool of the day,

*and they hid from the L*ORD *God*

among the trees of the garden.

Genesis 3:8

"MADE FOR A WOMAN. STRONG ENOUGH FOR A MAN"

It's a paradox. It seems impossible to be strong, yet soft. But that's exactly what the makers of women's deodorant Secret have set out to do. Their slogan (the section title) captures the idea of how the perfect feminine antiperspirant functions. It fights off bad while producing good. It's a gross example, but it works.

This is essentially what husbands are called to do. Married men are to be tough toward sin yet tender in respect to nurturing their wives. They are to be stable and consistent emotional supports for their spouses. They are to be strong like men (1 Corinthians 16:13), though they were made to nourish women (Ephesians 5:28–29).

Here's another example: a husband being simultaneously soft and strong with his wife is like punching through a stack of bricks while preserving an egg inside of his fist. Though it seems counterintuitive, it's possible. In fact, Jackie Chan can punch through slabs of cement while holding an egg in his fist, leaving the shell completely intact. Look it up on YouTube. You don't have to be Asian to do it, but that would probably help.

An argument can be made that being a consistently soft yet strong husband is more difficult than Chan's act. But a certain verse comes to mind: "But [Jesus] said, 'What is impossible with man is possible with God'" (Luke 18:27). A Spirit-filled husband who cares about reflecting Christ in his marriage will find everything he needs for godly living in God's Word (2 Peter 1:3).

LIVING ANTI-APATHETICALLY

Jesus is the standard for empathy. This is evidenced in the gospel itself. Romans 5:6 says, "For while we were still weak, at the right time Christ died for the ungodly." When men were estranged from God, Jesus stepped in to bridge the gap and make a way for the lost to be reconciled to their Creator. He would have been perfectly just to write men off—but He had divine compassion on the enemies of God.

Thinking back about how Adam hid with Eve in the garden, it can be said that his actions were nothing if not un-Christlike. There's no way that he could have been his wife's ultimate savior, but he certainly could have led her to repentance. Instead, his response to the situation was to hide. He wanted to pretend as though the Lord didn't know about his shortcomings and his reaction was to bury himself in his own shame, dragging his wife down with him.

Unfortunately, that scenario is not unique to the first married couple. In fact, this happens frequently today. Husbands and wives sin against God and against each other, then bury their wickedness deep down in their hearts, refusing to admit guilt or commit to change. They think God is like them—foolish and weak. The truth is that He is the opposite, so He would lovingly receive them and change their hearts if they would only turn from their own evil.

For you, the Christian husband, living anti-apathetically means two things: being sensitive to your own sin and being sensitive to your wife's well-being—in that order. If a husband holds back sin in his heart, storing it deep down and refusing to repent, he will be unable to lead his wife emotionally or spiritually. He must come clean in regards to his own shortcomings and he must be empathetic.

A GLIMPSE OF CHRIST'S TENDERNESS

Luke, the famous doctor of the New Testament who wrote one of the four gospels, gives Bible readers a unique look into the compassion of Jesus. At the end of chapter seven, Luke writes this:

> One of the Pharisees asked him to eat with him, and he went into the Pharisee's house and reclined at the table. And behold, a woman of the city, who was a sinner, when she learned that he was reclining at table in the Pharisee's house, brought an alabaster flask of ointment, and standing behind him at his feet, weeping, she began to wet his feet with her tears and wiped them with the hair of her head and kissed his feet and anointed them with the ointment. Now when the Pharisee who had invited him saw this, he said to himself, "If this man were a prophet, he would have known who and what sort of woman this is who is touching him, for she is a sinner."

> Then turning toward the woman he said to Simon, "Do you see this woman? I entered your house; you gave me no water for my feet, but she has wet my feet with her tears and wiped them with her hair. You gave me no kiss, but from the time I came in she has not ceased to kiss my feet. You did not anoint my head with oil, but she has anointed my feet with ointment. Therefore I tell you, her sins, which are many, are forgiven—for she loved much." (vv. 36–39, 44–47a)

Skimming through this story 2,000 years after it happened is not enough to inspire the typical male. So to get the most out of this account, men must think deeply about the context of the interaction.

The story begins with Jesus accepting a Pharisee's invitation to dinner. That alone is mind-bending. God doesn't have to put up with self-righteous narcissists, but all sinners should be thankful that He does. He has incredible mercy and patience.

What happens next, though, is unexpected. A woman shows up. She's broken, emotionally needy, and full of faith. She could have gone to many different men—but she chose Jesus. She knew that the Christ had come and her only hope was in Him. As she enters the house, her actions reveal her heart. She begins to lovingly serve Jesus while He (presumably) was in the middle of conversation with this stubborn Pharisee.

Two men are meeting together. One of them is all-powerful, all-knowing, and perfectly pure. The other is a cold, hard, religious man of little faith. These men are talking to each other when an annoying pest (as many men would have viewed a woman at that time) comes timidly into the room. The natural instinct of the carnal man is to get the dirty discomfort out of the way.

But Jesus isn't carnal. He's God.

So as the Pharisee proceeds to openly put the woman to shame, Christ turns the tables and exposes the Pharisee's heart for what it is—an unclean mess. He shows the cold man his cold heart.

Similar instances pop up from time to time in marriage. Husbands are tired and/or distracted when their wives come into the picture in a very needy way. Your wife may have had a bad day with the kids or a frustrating experience at the grocery store; either way, she needs you—the most important man in her life—to listen to her and give her your attention.

However, we men don't always pull through. Phrases like, "Why are you crying?" or "Do we have to talk about this now?"

The apostle Peter writes, "Husbands, live with your wives in an understanding way, showing honor to the woman as the weaker vessel, since they are heirs with you of the grace of life, so that your prayers may not be hindered" (1 Peter 3:7). The term *weaker* tends to initiate knee-jerk reactions in the church today, but it can be easily explained and understood. Women are physically weaker than men (or, at least, they typically are) and have physiological complexities that make them physically and emotionally needier than their male counterparts.

As far as those complexities are concerned, the area of emotions stands out as more noticeable than the rest. Women are soft, sensitive, and sincere. Men are stiff, strong, and tend to be sarcastic. Husbands aren't told to change who they are—they're told to live with their wives in an understanding way.

KEEPING IT UNDER CONTROL

In the quest for peaceful enjoyment within the confines of marriage, men must take control of the emotional energy within the relationship. Men need to be available and gentle with their wives while not allowing feelings to dictate what truth is or become an excuse for sin. As important as it is to absorb a woman's feelings through diligent listening, responsiveness, and encouragement, it is just as important to keep those feelings in check.

Many marriages are led by the way the wife feels. This is tragic indeed. The man is afraid to take control because the woman "just *knows*" in her heart (i.e., the emotional center in her brain) that this or that is God's desire. Women—just like men—sometimes can and will be wrong. It's the husband's job to let his wife know when her feelings are out of line. Do not fear the prospect of correcting your bride.

Ephesians 5:26 says that husbands are to imitate Christ by sanctifying their wives by the washing of the Word. Men need to be firm in their conviction of truth as found in Scripture. Gently, lovingly, and graciously, with strength, husbands need to lead in their homes with the truth of Scripture. It is only in this way that men of God can complete the task of being the emotional leader. This topic cannot be overstressed. You must find the balance between listener and leader. It's not an either/or proposition—it's a both/and commission! Listen to the wife of your youth; comfort her and nourish her. As you do these things, do not let her emotional decisions guide the home. Maintain the position God has given you by exercising compassionate fortitude. If emotions are dictating what your family will or will not do, the home will self-implode. Truth must override every whimsy; feelings must give way to God. It's your job to keep that in order under your roof.

There's a delicate balance to all this. On the one hand, we men can be tempted to turn into a military general who answers his wife's emotional pleas with curt, stiff responses. On the other hand, we can be tempted to get passive and keep our mouth shut as she follows Eve's poor example in discernment.

You must be a man who nurtures his wife. It requires patience, ambition, and wheelbarrow-loads of prayer to fulfill the role God gave you—but you can do it. He'll help you.

A PLAN OF ACTION

Big Idea: Men are called to be emotionally stable. It's up to the Christian husband to be simultaneously soft and strong, while keeping emotions in check in the home. **Assignment**: Have a wise man evaluate your personal emotional stability. Tell him to be painfully honest. If you know you're a bit unstable, you need to be courageous about this and risk the chance of crying in front of another man.

- Take another courageous step and ask your wife how good of a listener you are. Correct as needed.

- Talk with her about the relationship between emotions and truth. Make sure you bring it up every few weeks and keep a close watch on how it all plays out at home. Again, correct as needed.

- As often as you can without the moment feeling forced, contrived, or cursory, try ending your day by complimenting your wife on something she's doing well. Give her the affirmation she craves and deserves. As you're lying there in bed, just before you say, "I love you" and roll over, let her know what you've observed that she really does well.

YOU ARE THE LOVER

Therefore a man shall leave his father

and his mother

and hold fast to his wife,

and they shall become one flesh.

And the man and his wife were both naked

and were not ashamed.

Genesis 2:24–25

THE BEDROOM AS THE LOCKER ROOM

"It's one of the last things we talk about," says Ted Thompson, the general manager of the Green Bay Packers, about the football team's locker room.

"The locker room is an extraordinarily important part of the organization and, I think, your success," he continued. "All of a sudden you have a bad guy in the locker room, that's worse than having a bad player."[8]

The locker room is the place where guys can chat and relax, discuss life's problems, and become real friends. On the field, it's all business. The guys are on the job and busy fulfilling very specific roles. But in the locker room, everything is more dressed down (pun intended) and the athletes can get to know each other on a

---

8   Tyler Dunne, "NFL locker rooms are built using varying styles of brick," Milwaukee Journal-Sentinel, http://archive.jsonline.com/sports/nfl-locker-rooms-are-built-using-varying-styles-of-brick-b99213305z1-247182441.html.

personal level. To use a very emasculating word, the setting is much more *intimate*. (Shiver.)

Married couples need to take a page out of Thompson's playbook here. Husbands and wives may not have locker rooms in their home, but they have something much more intimate and certainly more important: their bedrooms.

The word *bedroom*, of course, is used as a euphemism for sexual intimacy between a man and his wife. Like the locker room, it is often one of the last things that gets talked about, because talk between spouses concerning sex is often surrounded with shame or embarrassment rather than enthusiasm and excitement. Also like the locker room, the bedroom is an extraordinarily important part of success in marriage. It directly affects morale and can often shape the way spouses view each other.

Of course, there are major differences between the locker room and the bedroom. The locker room is full of sweaty and hairy dudes, and the bedroom features just one Neanderthal-like creature (you) and your soft, sweet-smelling wife. Aren't you glad that God has given you a woman? Imagine what life would be like if you had to live with someone like yourself! (Another shiver!)

What happens in the marriage bed is of extreme importance, as it can be a helpful barometer of the relationship. Barometers tell of the atmospheric pressure as either falling/deteriorating or rising/ improving. These same measurements can be applied to any given couple's marriage union through their sex lives. A good sex life is often evidence of a good marriage. And more sex does not equal a good sex life. More on that later.

NOT GIVE-AND-TAKE, BUT GIVE-AND-GIVE

It has been said (by unwise individuals) that marriage is a "give-and-take" kind of relationship. Spouses can give some and take some, they say; they can take out of the relationship what they put into it. That statement not only encourages a wrong motivation for fulfilling God's design, but when it is applied to sex it also puts unfair expectations on a person's spouse.

First Corinthians 7:3–4 (NLT) says this: "The husband should fulfill his wife's sexual needs, and the wife should fulfill her husband's needs. The wife gives authority over her body to her husband, and the husband gives authority over his body to his wife."

Notice the apostle is not saying "Take what is rightfully yours"; rather, he expresses a short command: "fulfill." Paul's words to married couples convey a sense of freedom and generosity in the bedroom. He goes on to say, "Do not deprive one another . . . so that Satan may not tempt you because of your lack of self-control" (v. 5).

Sex is about generosity. Problems in the bed are actually problems of the heart—problems of gratuity. It's perhaps an uncomfortable thought (this chapter is full of uncomfortable thoughts), but your servant's-heart is put on display in the bedroom just as much as it is anywhere else. If a husband is selfish in bed, it's just as clear a manifestation of pride as when he's selfish in other places. Jesus said, "It is more blessed to give than to receive" (Acts 20:35), and this statement is true in all contexts where a person can positively influence another. When it comes to sex, men in particular need to view themselves as the servants rather than the kings and masters who expect their wives to serve them.

This idea is all the more important when considering your wife's background. Regardless of her former lifestyle—whether she was someone who "got around" a little bit or she was a goodie-two-shoes—she is bringing into your bed a perspective that is unique to her. She might be nervous on the first night of the honeymoon and, if you act like a slave master instead of a servant under the sheets, she might remain nervous for years. She might be excited to do things she wants to do in the bedroom, but if you try to control her, she may clam up. As in the other areas of life, trust takes large chunks of time to earn but only a moment to lose. You do not want to mess these things up.

PORN HAS PROBABLY BROKEN YOUR BRAIN

Here are some statistics to justify my subtitle:[9]

- 90% of children ages 8–16 have viewed pornography.

- The largest consumers of porn are 12- to 17-year old boys.

- 70% of men ages 18 to 34 visit a pornographic website in a typical month.

- 25% of search engine requests are pornography-related.

- Every second, 28,258 people view pornography.

- Every minute, $184,500 is spent on pornography.

Couple those with these similarly depressing stats:[10]

- 15% of married couples haven't had sex in six months or more.

- 59% of adults say extra-marital sexual thoughts/fantasies are acceptable.

- 38% of adults say pornography is morally acceptable.

Nearly all men (and the number increases with each generation) have viewed pornography. As noted above, most young men look at pornography regularly. Porn has messed up the thoughts, motivations, and expectations of young men. Unfortunately, this is not a "non-Christian" issue, it's very much an in-house discussion as it pertains to the Church. Millions of men willingly fall into the

---

9   http://www.guardchild.com/statistics and https://www.webroot.com/us/en/home/resources/tips/digital-family-life/internet-pornography-by-the-numbers.
10   Ibid.

porn trap and some of those who pledge allegiance to Christ are a part of the mix.

Here's a key point: pornography is not real. Sadly, many newly-married men think it *is* real and their mission is to re-enact with their unsuspecting wives all of the perversions they have seen in their past. Once reality sets in, though, the men often feel a bitter disappointment that their wives don't understand why they want to do this. This situation leads to inevitable frustration and the married couple's sex life only goes downhill from there.

The main idea is this: men and their wives should set their standard of expectations together. As noted above, though, the bedroom, like a locker room, is rarely discussed by couples. But husbands need to talk to their spouses about sex. It has to happen. The conversation needs to be approached from a mindset of servanthood, not from selfishness, and the man and wife should build their own standard of sexual expectations. False images of pornography need to be destroyed and the only way to diminish them is for a man to turn to the woman God has blessed him with for complete sexual fulfillment.

Additionally, spouses need to find their standard of beauty wholly in each other. It is incredibly tempting to adapt standards of beauty from what is seen on the internet, television, or in real life. A married person might observe an attractive individual and think, "Why can't my spouse be like *that*?!" But that's idolatry. That's adultery. That's sin. Whatever a person's spouse is like (physical features, personality, etc.), that is what the person should regard as perfect human beauty.

Think about your wife right now. How tall is she? What color is her hair? What's her build? What makes her laugh? What does she love to do?

You can't beat that. She's your standard of humanly beauty. Your wife is the best you could ever have.

That's not to say that there are no attractive people except for your spouse. It would be foolish to say that nobody besides your wife is objectively attractive. That kind of thinking leads to dangerous ends as well. If a man gets so worried about thinking of any other women as attractive, his thoughts will soon be consumed by images of other women—the very thing he doesn't want to think about!

In Philippians 4:8, Paul says that Christians should think about "whatever is true, whatever is honorable, whatever is just, whatever is pure, whatever is lovely, whatever is commendable." He goes on to say in the same verse, "if there is any excellence, if there is anything worthy of praise, think about these things." The wife God has given you meets the standard for one of the awesome things you can think about. Don't go to one extreme or the other thinking about other women.

MAKE LOVE, MAKE KIDS, MAKE FUN

Intercourse is obviously designed for reproduction. God said to Adam and Eve, "Be fruitful and multiply"—and He didn't mean by way of adoption (Genesis 1:28). However, sex is not just for reproduction. An entire book of the Bible, the Song of Solomon, shows that within the confines of heterosexual marriage, sex can and should be quite recreational. The book is packed with make-you-blush descriptions from the bedroom—and there's no mention of any children!

Some verses in the Song of Solomon are quite straightforward in their expression of recreational lovemaking within marriage. Perhaps it's best to share some verses without providing specific interpretation:

As an apple tree among the trees of the forest,

so is my beloved among the young men.

With great delight I sat in his shadow,

and his fruit was sweet to my taste. (2:3)

Your lips drip nectar, my bride;

honey and milk are under your tongue;

the fragrance of your garments

is like the fragrance of Lebanon. (4:11)

It's possible that the biggest hurdle many conservative married couples face is the idea that they can have sex recreationally. Several women who come from conservative families were not just protected from sinful expressions of sex—but from any knowledge of sex altogether. When young men marry these women and are ready to satisfy the desires they have been suppressing for some time, the brides are not always ready to "party." It's the husband's job to be understanding (remember 1 Peter 3:7?) and to serve his wife, as the couple arrives at enjoyable, biblical conclusions in their bedroom.

As leaders, men need to keep these ideas in balance. While sex can be used for both reproduction and for recreation, it is not solely designated for either. It can be purposed for conception, it can be purposed for pure enjoyment, but ultimately it needs to be done out of a loving heart. The act of sex brings men and women closer together in unimaginable ways. It's the reason why sex complicates things for two unmarried people; it's why God has reserved it only for the ones who have entered into a covenant. The way physical baptism reflects an individual's spiritual baptism that takes place in their heart, the physical union of a man and his wife reflects the one-flesh spiritual union that takes place at the moment the couple says, "I do."

Sex is a gift. It's exciting, personal, and fulfilling. But just like every other worthwhile endeavor, it takes work and requires sacrifice. Men should set the tone of servitude in their marriage and find a balance for the sake of their marital relationship. Remember, women are put in an incredibly vulnerable position in nearly every aspect of marriage; the bedroom is arguably where she's the *most* vulnerable. It does no good for you, her, or your relationship as a whole to be pushy, demanding, selfish, ungrateful, or grumpy in the bedroom.

One more note: Numerous sources will try to tell you that having sex *x-number* of times per week will make everything better in your relationship. That's simply not true. Every couple is different, because every person is different. There are some guys (okay, most guys) who would like to make love to their wife six days a week. There are some women (okay, most women) who are fine with six days a month. Variables abound in situations like this and you simply have to discover what's best for you and your wife. Don't try to force a solution that's inconsiderate of your spouse's unique needs.

A good sex-life is not based on numbers alone, and you must discuss these possibly uncomfortable conversation topics with your bride. If she's comfortable in bed, you'll both be better off. She's got so many pressures to deal with day in and day out; make sure you alleviate this one by being a humble servant.

Love her. Serve her. Have fun.

A PLAN OF ACTION

Big Idea: God has given you instructions for sex. There are multiple purposes for it; however, your role in it is not unlike your role in every other area of marriage. You're a humble servant who should strive to make his wife happy and godlier.

Assignment: This one is pretty simple. If you've not had a conversation with your wife about sex, have one. Ask her if she's comfortable. Find out if there's anything you need to change. Have the conversation multiple times a year as needed. You'll be a better husband for it.

YOU ARE THE MANAGER

The LORD God took the man

and put him in the garden of Eden

to work it and keep it.

Genesis 2:15

A CALL TO THE BULLPEN

In the middle of big cities there exists a pastoral game that takes place all summer long. Large stadiums for playing this game are built surrounding a patch of grass and dirt about three acres in size. Grown men scurry around like children, running, jumping, and swinging bats, seeking to score more runs than the opposition.

Unless you're from another planet, you know that the sport is baseball (otherwise known as the best of all sports). What you may not know is that an integral part of the game is the bullpen. There are certain players whose only job is to take the pitcher's mound any time a situation occurs that requires their unique skill set. The modern function of the bullpen evolved during the 1970s and 80s, when then-Oakland A's manager Tony LaRussa started using bullpen pitchers for just one batter—maybe even just one pitch—if the situation called for it.

LaRussa's greatest invention, the one that changed the game of baseball the most, was the *closer*. *Closers* are the most dominant, confident pitchers, who must have nerves of steel in order to do their job. Their responsibility is to come into the game near the very end when their teams are winning, and not let the other team score any more runs. They have to close the door and secure the victory, whether their team is ahead by three runs or just one. Much like place kickers in football, the whole game depends on them, even if they're only on the field for a few minutes.

Christian husbands are called to be closers. Through the ins and outs of their lives, day-to-day decisions have to be made that must be executed properly. However, many choices you'll be faced with really don't match your skill set. In this way, you are also called to be a manager. A man has to be a closer and seal the deal, but he also has to be a manager and get the right help for the task at hand.

What's the best way to build up a savings account? What should be looked for in a used car? Whose family gets visited on what holidays? How do you stop a leaky faucet? How can more money be saved at the grocery store? Is it better to have a 401(k) or Roth IRA?

There are very few men who can give immediate, perfect answers to each of these questions. The ones who can give good answers more than likely learned the answers over time, by interacting with people who were more or less experts in those respected fields. (You should go with the Roth IRA, by the way . . . rhyme intentional).

Enter the bullpen. Young Christian husbands will be faced with many decisions in the first few years of marriage. Many of the questions seem impossible to answer correctly, as the thought of making the wrong choice puts a great amount of stress on the man. To alleviate that stress, he must make a call to the bullpen.

The closers of baseball, though dominant, can do only so much. Typically, they're just standard pitchers who throw the ball very, very hard. Other guys in the bullpen might be lefty sidearm guys or right-handers who can throw something odd like the slurve (slider + curve). A middle reliever might have a knuckleball in his arsenal or perhaps a particularly devastating changeup that locks up the batter every time. Those unique skills are not typical of closers. Closers throw plain old fastballs well over half of the time. The fastball is a speedy, direct pitch that doesn't involve much confusion. It's an exclamation point. It's an emphatic I'm-going-to-end-this way to finalize the game.

Closers don't get themselves to that point in the game, though—they can't. They rely on the rest of the bullpen. Throughout the rest of this chapter, the husband will be viewed as both the closer and the manager. His resources are found in his bullpen. The proverbial game—his marriage—is on the line. It's time to close it out.

TAKING THE REINS

Not all men are good with numbers; not all men are good with cars; most men don't understand shopping; nearly every man would rather spend a day doing one of his hobbies than shooting the breeze with his in-laws. However, husbands have to make solid decisions in these areas (along with others) to the benefit of their marriages.

In order to be a successful manager in his marriage, a Christian husband must develop a garrison (bullpen) of solid resources that he can turn to when a decision is required. Most times, the resource will be another man, a guy who has proven himself to be wise in a certain area of life. When a baseball manager needs to strike out a left-handed power hitter, he'll go to his bullpen and bring in the lefty with a hard slider. When a Christian man needs advice on how to invest money, he needs to call on the man in his church who has successful experience in that regard.

In order for this concept to make sense, you must say something to yourself now and multiple times in the future. It's a very important statement that you must believe in order to be a successful manager. If you don't buy into this, you will find yourself getting frustrated at every turn. Here's the statement: "There's a lot I don't know."

Every good manager knows that he is insufficient in and of himself to do his job well. Keeping with the baseball analogy, there's a reason why the major league manager has a pitching coach, hitting coach, bench manager, and trainer on his staff. He absolutely can't do it all. He is unable to be proficient in all areas—and he's not expected to be. You're not expected to do it all, either. Admit it to yourself time and time again: there's a lot you don't know.

In the following sub-sections, we'll look at different areas of managerial leadership in order to get a better grasp on what a husband must be prepared for in his marriage.

SCHEDULING

Life—especially in 2017—runs on a strict schedule. The more children a couple has, the fuller and more complicated the schedule becomes. If a man doesn't know what his wife is doing, where she is, or when she will be doing something, he will most certainly lose touch with his entire family. This doesn't just apply to day-to-day time slots; men need to be involved in the big picture concepts as much as they are involved with the little details of everything else.

Husbands must have an agenda. Scripture says, "For the husband is the head of the wife even as Christ is the head of the church" (Ephesians 5:23a). The church does not set the schedule, but it appeals to God in all of their plans (James 4:13–15). Husbands are not called to be as sovereign over their schedules as God is over the church's plans, but they are the ones responsible to manage the affairs of their homes.

Men are to be so involved that they have a vision for themselves, their marriage, and their entire household. In fact, if they don't, they're not cut out for church leadership. First Timothy 3:5 asks, "For if someone does not know how to manage his own household, how will he care for God's church?" The word used for *manage* means "to rule over, preside, direct, lead by example." That's the role of a baseball manager and, more importantly, it's the Christian husband's calling.

FINANCES

There are few areas in a marriage that cause more stress than the realm of finances. Sometimes the husband and wife come into their relationship with different philosophies of household economics. One person may be quite frugal, while the other sees every paycheck as a personal stimulus bill that must be put back into the local economy as soon as possible. When these two ideas clash, it can become frustrating on both ends.

To make things even more complicated, one of you (or both of you) may have brought debt into marriage. Maybe you have different philosophies of debt. How will a sticky money situation be reconciled?

The answer to this is to make the more fiscally responsible spouse the keeper of the checkbook. If both spouses in a marriage are honest with themselves, they can easily recognize which person in the relationship is better overall with allocating, spending, and managing money. Some men are not wired to punch keys on a calculator but their wives are. Others readily volunteer for it with their wives' greatest blessing. And yet some husbands have no choice but to step up, because neither they nor their wives have a desire for it.

Greg Baker says it well: "Many Christian men worry that they are forfeiting in-home leadership if they delegate certain financial responsibilities to their wives, even when their wives are better suited for the detailed rigors of budgeting . . . a Christian husband should not feel the least bit threatened by his wife's involvement in their personal finances. Perhaps hubby is better suited to manage the budgetary details. If so, that's wonderful. But he should always seek consensus from his wife regarding their financial goals and, perhaps even more importantly, he should always heed her cautions."[11]

No matter what each spouse's personal desires are in a given household, their finances must be properly controlled. Irresponsible spending is not a righteous thing and it is a bad testimony to the world. Proverbs 3:9 makes a simple statement: "Honor the Lord with your wealth." This is the Christian family's goal.

What this also means is that the husband is the provider. First Timothy 5:8 says, talking to men: "But if anyone does not provide for his relatives, and especially for members of his household, he has denied the faith and is worse than an unbeliever." That's a smack in the face for the guys who are too lazy to get to work. If that means flipping burgers, rounding up grocery carts, or working the register at Best Buy, then so be it. A man shouldn't hold down the couch while his wife stresses over an empty checking account. He also shouldn't hold out for a management position at the expense of his family's well-being.

QUALITY PURCHASES

Perhaps an un-thought-of area of management has to do with the quality of items purchased for the family. For instance, if the family needs a new car and has a meager $3,000 dollars to spend, what plan of action does the husband take? He could look for a car that's $3,000 or less; he could use that $3,000 as a down payment on a more expensive and reliable car; he could also leave the decision up to his wife. The last choice is not really an option.

Those kinds of choices are hard, but they come up frequently for many young married couples. The big idea is that the man needs to make sure he doesn't squander what the family has for the sake of "getting by." Sticking with the car example, the husband might

---

11   Greg Baker, "Finances in Marriage: His or Hers?", *Rooted Thinking* blog, January 15, 2016, http://rootedthinking.com/2016/01/15/finances-in-mar-riage-his-or-hers/.

find a car for $2,995 that ends up costing them an additional $2,500 in repairs in the long run. That was not a quality purchase and it put his family in a bind.

Husbands, as the family's leader, will need to call on their bullpen in instances such as this when they pop up. Decision-making isn't about finding a piece that fits in the puzzle and making it work. It's about finding the piece that goes with each particular puzzle and completing the big picture of God's design. This requires wisdom from God, which He gives generously (James 1:5), as well as help from brothers and sisters in the faith.

MAINTENANCE

Appliances are designed to break. Years ago, washers, dryers, microwaves, and the like were all made to last for more than a decade before they showed signs of wear and tear (they were made in America, too . . . perhaps there's a correlation). These days, though, household tools are made cheaply and are replaced relatively cheaply. Some little plastic piece inside of them will break, causing the whole appliance to become worthless. Oftentimes they need to be replaced more than they need fixed.

Other items, such as vehicles or houses, are much more complex and need actual maintenance. Lawns, walls, windows, carpets, and the like, all need to be maintained in order to keep up appearances and function as they should. Maintenance requires a mindful and purposeful steward.

Husbands are the chief stewards of their homes. In the parable of the dishonest manager, Jesus says, "One who is faithful in a very little is also faithful in much, and one who is dishonest in a very little is also dishonest in much. If then you have not been faithful in the unrighteous wealth, who will entrust to you the true riches?" (Luke 16:10–11). God desires that men take care of that which He has given them to manage.

If a man's house is falling apart—if the washer has been broken for weeks and his wife has to go the laundromat, weeds have overtaken the flower bed, the junk in the garage keeps the cars in the driveway—he is failing. The man must own up to his responsibility as a household manager by maintaining that which is under his care. To the best of his ability, a husband should make sure the vehicles are all in good condition, the house is presentable, and that everything is functioning.

LEADING CHILDREN

Over the course of a marriage, men and women add to their family by way of procreation. Rugrats start appearing, eating, growing, and rebelling. They need to be led spiritually and physically. They need an involved male presence. Not all of this has to do with teaching them the Bible (though this is of utmost importance—read Ephesians 6:4).

Decisions have to be made about how the children will be schooled, how they'll be involved in the community, what books and movies they'll be allowed to read and watch, etc. Husbands need to lead conversations about these things with their wives. If men turn a blind eye to their children's lives, they have lost all perspective. The chief ministry of a man is his family.

A husband being involved in the lives of his children includes disciplining them. Proverbs 13:24 says, "Whoever spares the rod hates his son, but he who loves him is diligent to discipline him." Contemporary American culture says that children should be given liberties that would have been unthinkable a few decades ago—let alone at the time of the writing of Proverbs. The role of a husband/father is to lead his children by disciplining them with love. He must be intimately involved in the lives of each person who resides under his roof.

MANAGE. CLOSE

Thinking back to the baseball analogy, husbands are called to manage their families as baseball managers lead their teams. You are called to strategize, cast a vision, encourage, inspire, and take responsibility. You're also the closer. You're the one who steps into the game when the big decision needs to be made. You're called to emphatically, deliberately, and intentionally make decisions and choices that seal the deal. When it's all on the line, the husband's role is to step up.

God has called you to a high responsibility. You're to plan, manage, and see both big projects and small tasks through to completion. The Lord enables you to do all of this through His Word and by His Spirit. Strive to manage well.

A PLAN OF ACTION

Big Idea: You've been placed in a position of management. Seek helpful counselors, make good plans, and execute them with wisdom.

Assignment: Seek out wise men who can assist you with the various matters of life. These categories may include the following:

- Finances

- Various types of repairs

- Relationships

- Organization and time management

- Real estate

Admit that you don't know everything. Call on these men as necessary so that you can make good decisions for your family.

SET YOUR MIND ON THINGS ABOVE

For you have died,
and your life is hidden
with Christ in God.

Colossians 3:3

I was sixteen years old when I was saved by Christ. There were so many things to learn at that point in my life. I essentially knew nothing about the Bible, and all the church stuff was foreign to me. God placed several good men in my life, though, and I began to understand more and more about the gospel and the nature of my Savior. One of the first bits of wisdom I ever learned was a simple phrase: "There is a God and you're not Him."

In a sense, that was all I needed to know at that time. I needed a proper perspective—and a constant reminder—concerning the greatness of God and the wretchedness of man. In the same way, the apostle Paul reminds the Colossian believers of the perspective they were called to have. They had died and their lives were hidden with Christ in God. The words that were written and preserved by God Himself are still just as applicable for us today.

You have died. Let the idea sink in for a moment.

Elsewhere in Scripture, Paul puts it this way: "I have been crucified with Christ. It is no longer I who live, but Christ who lives in me" (Galatians 2:20a).

You're dead. Christ is the One living in you.

If the defense lawyer in your mind is making a case as to why you cannot or should not be the husband God wants you to be, let biblical truth pound him into submission. Your old, prideful self—the self that makes sure you're the most important person in your life—is dead. Your old man was crucified; your old man is dead. Paul went on to say, "And the life I now live in the flesh I live by faith in the Son of God, who loved me and gave himself for me" (Galatians 2:20b). This means that your new life has purpose. The Christian life is designed to be lived for Christ Himself—to be full of servanthood, grace, mercy, humility, and wisdom.

You can live that life.

God's Spirit has been sent into your heart so that you may call out to Him, "Abba, Father!" (Romans 8:15). He empowers you to be loving, joyful, peaceful, patient, kind, good, faithful, gentle, and controlled (Galatians 5:22–23). He's placed a sword in your hand—the word of God (Ephesians 6:17). He is completely God and He is yours. You are a slave who has all of the power in the universe because God lives in you. There are no excuses for sidestepping manly Christian responsibility.

In order to walk the walk of a Christian husband, you will have to continually set your mind on things above. Just before Paul told the Colossians that they had died (3:3), he reminded them to set their minds on things above, "not on things that are on the earth" (v. 2). That's the command—reject worldly thinking and focus on the heavenly. It's an imperative because of the death all Christians have experienced and the glorification that all Christians are awaiting. "When Christ who is your life appears, then you will also appear with him in glory" (v. 4). It only makes sense to focus on things of God.

There will be some very discouraging times in your marriage. There will be times when you think about unwanted and uncomfortable what-ifs. You'll wonder, "What if I would have married someone else?" and "What if I just reject all the Bible stuff and pursue the things I want?" There will be times (probably many times) when you'll believe the lie that you have the right to be angry—and you'll take it out on your wife.

During these times I hope you'll remember that you're told to act like a man (1 Corinthians 16:13). Men don't whine; men aren't selfish; men won't run from problems. You're the husband. You're a slave of Christ.

Go get 'em, men!

If we stand idly by, if we seek merely swollen, slothful ease and ignoble peace, if we shrink from the hard contests where men must win at hazard of their lives and at the risk of all they hold dear, then the bolder and stronger peoples will pass us by, and will win for themselves the domination of the world. Let us therefore boldly face the life of strife, resolute to do our duty well and manfully; resolute to uphold righteousness by deed and by word; resolute to be both honest and brave, to serve high ideals, yet to use practical methods. Above all, let us shrink from no strife, moral or physical, within or without the nation, provided we are certain that the strife is justified, for it is only through strife, through hard and dangerous endeavor, that we shall ultimately win the goal of true national greatness.

—Theodore Roosevelt, *The Strenuous Life*

For more information about

Jeremy Howard
and
You're the Husband
please visit:

www.jeremyhoward.net
jeremy@paysonbiblechurch.com
@jhow0089
www.facebook.com/jeremyhowardutah

For more information about
AMBASSADOR INTERNATIONAL
please visit:

www.ambassador-international.com
@AmbassadorIntl
www.facebook.com/AmbassadorIntl